Greatest
WORKS of ART
coloring book

Digital Creative Publishing

Author
Arthwr Bass

Editor
Vanessa Lozada Gil

Design and layout
Digital Creative Publishing

Images and photographs
Digital Creative Publishing
Creative Commons (CC) Public domain images

© Arthwr Bass, 2022
digitalcreativepublishing@gmail.com
Book aimed at students and art enthusiasts.
All rights reserved. The total or partial reproduction of this work is not allowed, nor its incorporation into a computer system, or its transmission in any form or by any means (electronic, mechanical, photocopy, recording, others) without previous and written authorization of the owners of the copyright. Infringement of these rights may constitute an offense against intellectual property.

The Happy Accidents of the Swing. Jean-Honoré Fragonard.

Table of contents

MAA'AT, EGYPTIAN GODDESS OF TRUTH 4
EURYNOME, POTHOS , HIPPODAMIA,
EROS, IASO, AND ASTERIA 5
ADORATION OF THE MAGI 6
THE ARNOLFINI PORTRAIT 7
ST. GEORGE AND THE DRAGON 8
ANNUNCIATION 9
ALLEGORY OF SPRING 10
THE BIRTH OF VENUS 11
THE LAST SUPPER 12
THE LADY WITH THE ERMINE 14
MONA LISA 15
THE CREATION OF ADAM 16
TRIUMPH OF GALATEA 18
BACCHUS AND ARIADNE 19
THE (LITTLE) TOWER OF BABEL 20
THE BURIAL OF THE COUNT OF ORGAZ 21
MUSICIANS 22
STILL LIFE WITH GAME FOWL 23
SUSANNA AND THE ELDERS 24
THE LAUGHING CAVALIER 25
CHARLES I IN THREE POSITIONS 26
LAS MENINAS 27
THE GIRL WITH A PEARL EARRING 28
MR. AND MRS. ANDREWS 29
THE HAPPY ACCIDENTS OF THE SWING 30
THE LADIES WALDEGRAVE 31
PORTRAIT OF A GENTLEMAN SKATING 32
NAPOLEON CROSSING THE ALPS 33
GRANDE ODALISQUE 34
THE WANDERER ABOVE THE SEA OF FOG .. 35
SATURN DEVOURING HIS SON 36
THE LIBERTY LEADING THE PEOPLE 37
THE GREAT WAVE OFF KANAGAWA 38

THE ANGELUS 39
THE KISS 40
OLYMPIA 41
THE BIRTH OF VENUS 42
MU BRIGADE, 6TH GROUP
(ROKUBANGUMI) 43
WHISTLER'S MOTHER 44
A COTTON OFFICE IN NEW ORLEANS 45
PARIS STREET IN RAINY WEATHER 46
SUNDAY AFTERNOON ON THE ISLAND
OF LA GRANDE JATTE 47
CAFÉ TERRACE AT NIGHT 48
THE STARRY NIGHT 49
SELF-PORTRAIT WITHOUT BEARD 50
THE SCREAM 51
FLAMING JUNE 52
THE SLEEPING GYPSY 53
LARGE BATHERS 54
A FRIEND IN NEED 55
THE KISS 56
LES DEMOISELLES D'AVIGNON 57
FOXES 58
THREE MUSICIANS 59
COMPOSITION VIII 60
AMERICAN GOTHIC 61
THE PERSISTENCE OF MEMORY 62
THE WEEPING WOMAN 63
THE TWO FRIDAS 64
NIGHTHAWKS 65
THE TEMPTATION OF ST. ANTHONY 66
SHOT MARILYNS 67
THE SON OF MAN 68
WOMAN, BIRD, STAR 69
DANCERS AT THE BAR 70

Maa'at, Egyptian goddess of truth
Unknown artist
1255 B.C.
Wall painting inside the tomb (QV66) of Nefertari, Egypt.

Eurynome, Pothos, Hippodamia, Eros, Iaso, and Asteria
Unknown artist
400 B.C.
Greece.

Adoration of the Magi
Gentile da Fabriano
1423
Gallery degli Uffizi, Florence - Italy.

The Arnolfini portrait
Jan van Eyck
1434
National Gallery, London - England.

St. George and the dragon
Paolo Uccello
1470
National Gallery, London - England.

Annunciation
Leonardo da Vinci
1472
*Gallery degli Uffizi,
Florence - Italy.*

Allegory of Spring
Sandro Botticelli
1477-1482
Gallery degli Uffizi, Florence - Italy.

The birth of Venus
Sandro Botticelli
1485–1486
Gallery degli Uffizi, Florence - Italy.

The last supper
Leonardo da Vinci
1495–1498
*Church Santa Maria delle Grazie,
Milan - Italy.*

13

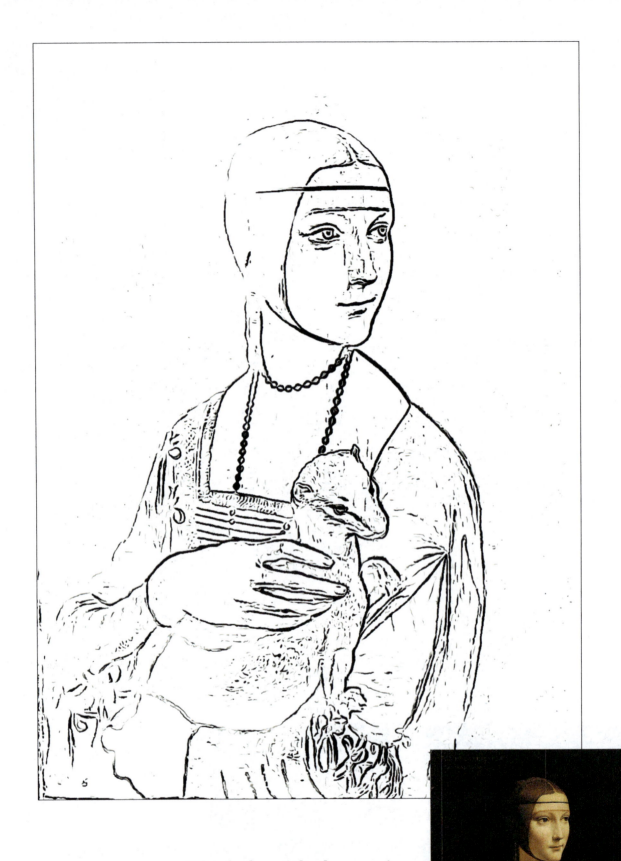

The lady with the ermine
Leonardo da Vinci
1489
Czartoryski Museum, Poland.

14

Mona Lisa
Leonardo da Vinci
1503
Louvre Museum, Paris - France.

The creation of Adam
Miguel Ángel
1511
*Sistine Chapel. Apostolic Palace,
Vatican City.*

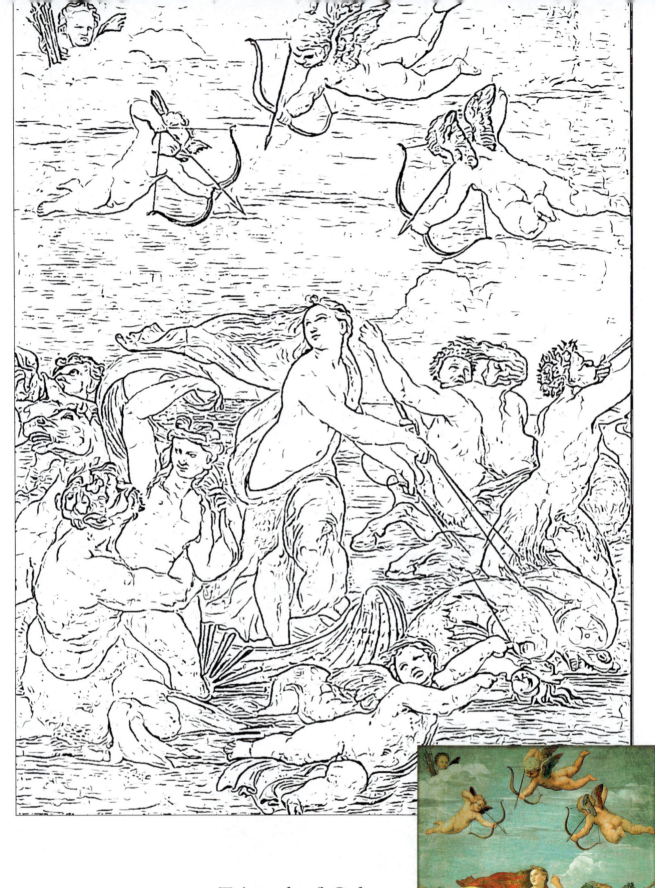

Triumph of Galatea
Rafael Sanzio
1511
Villa Farnesina, Rome - Italy.

Bacchus and Ariadne
Tiziano
1520
National Gallery, London - England.

The (Little) Tower of Babel
Pieter Brueghel el Viejo
1563
Boijmans Van Beuningen Museum, Rotterdam - The Netherlands.

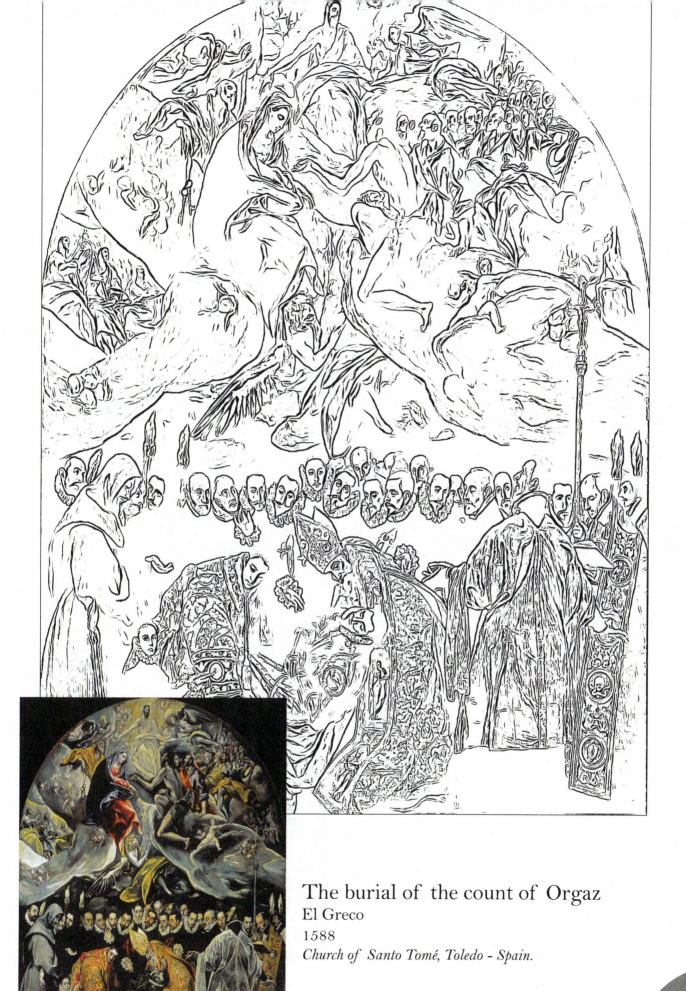

The burial of the count of Orgaz
El Greco
1588
Church of Santo Tomé, Toledo - Spain.

Musicians
Caravaggio
1595
*Metropolitan Museum of Art,
New York - United States.*

Still life with game fowl
Juan Sánchez Cotán
1600 - 1603
Instituto de Arte de Chicago, Estados Unidos.

Susanna and the elders
Artemisia Gentileschi
1610
Weißenstein Palace, Pommersfelden - Germany.

The laughing cavalier
Frans Hals
1624
Wallace Collection, London - England.

Charles I in three positions
Anton van Dyck
1635
Windsor Castle, UK.

Las meninas
Diego Velázquez
1656
Prado National Museum, Madrid - Spain.

The girl with a pearl earring
Johannes Vermeer
1665
Mauritshuis Museum in The Hague, Netherlands.

Mr. and Mrs. Andrews
Thomas Gainsborough
1750
National Gallery, London - England.

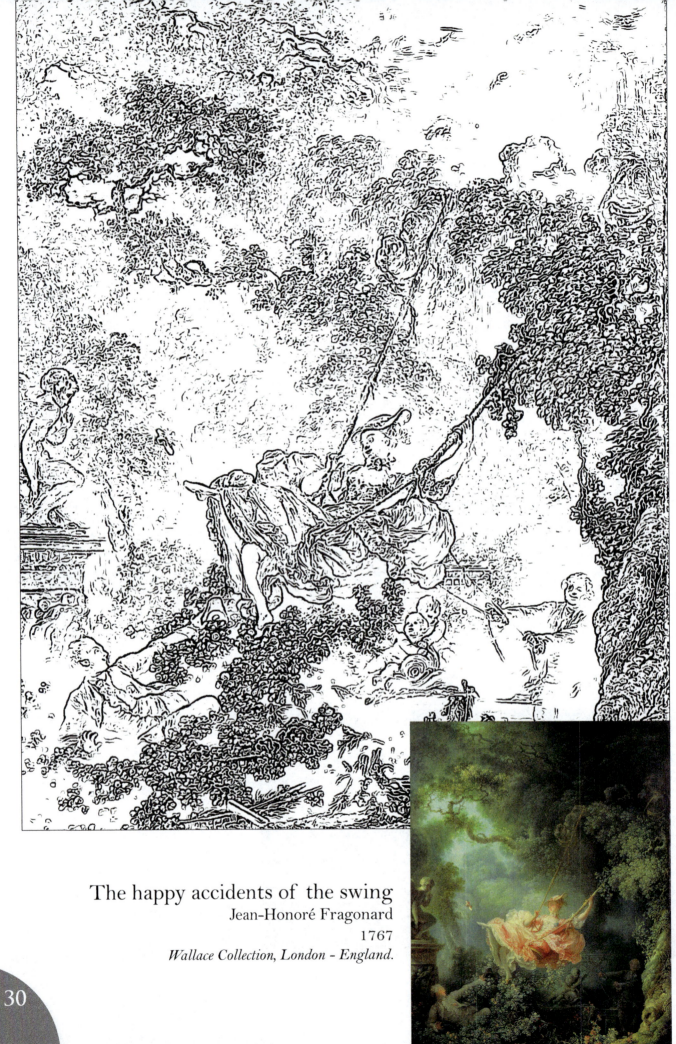

The happy accidents of the swing
Jean-Honoré Fragonard
1767
Wallace Collection, London - England.

The ladies Waldegrave
Joshua Reynolds
1780
National Gallery, Scotland.

Portrait of a gentleman skating
William Grant
1782
National Gallery of Art, Washington D.C. - United States.

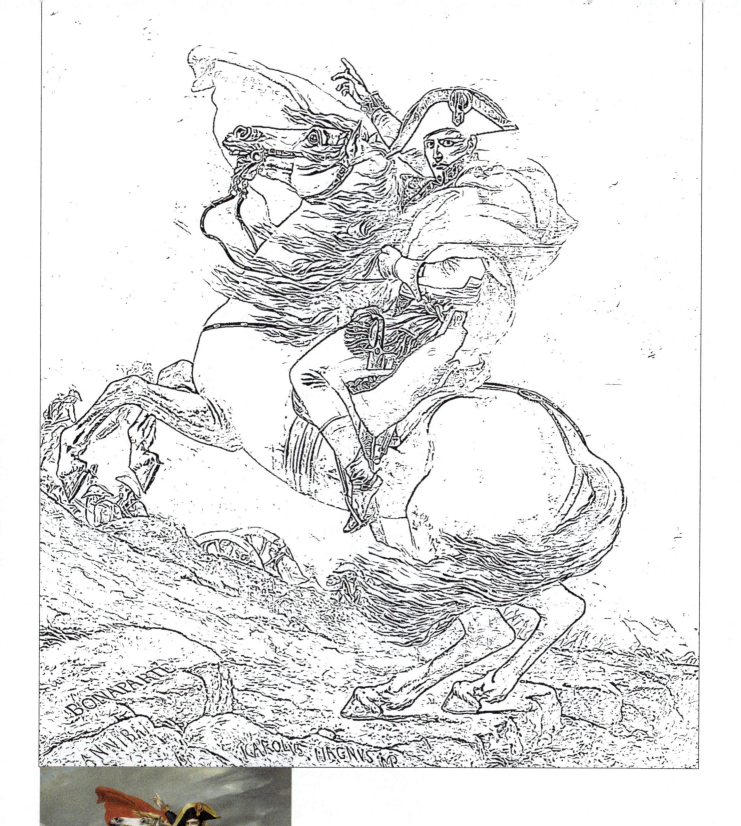

Napoleon crossing the Alps
Jacques-Louis David
1801–1805
Malmaison Castle, Rueil-Malmaison - France.

33

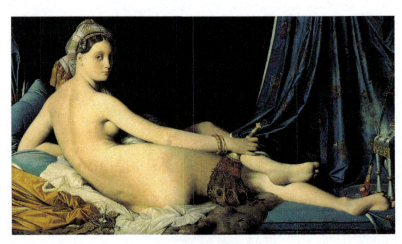

Grande Odalisque
Jean-Auguste-Dominique Ingres
1814
Louvre Museum, Paris - France.

The wanderer above the sea of fog
Caspar David Friedrich
1818
Art museum in Kunsthalle in Hamburg, Germany.

35

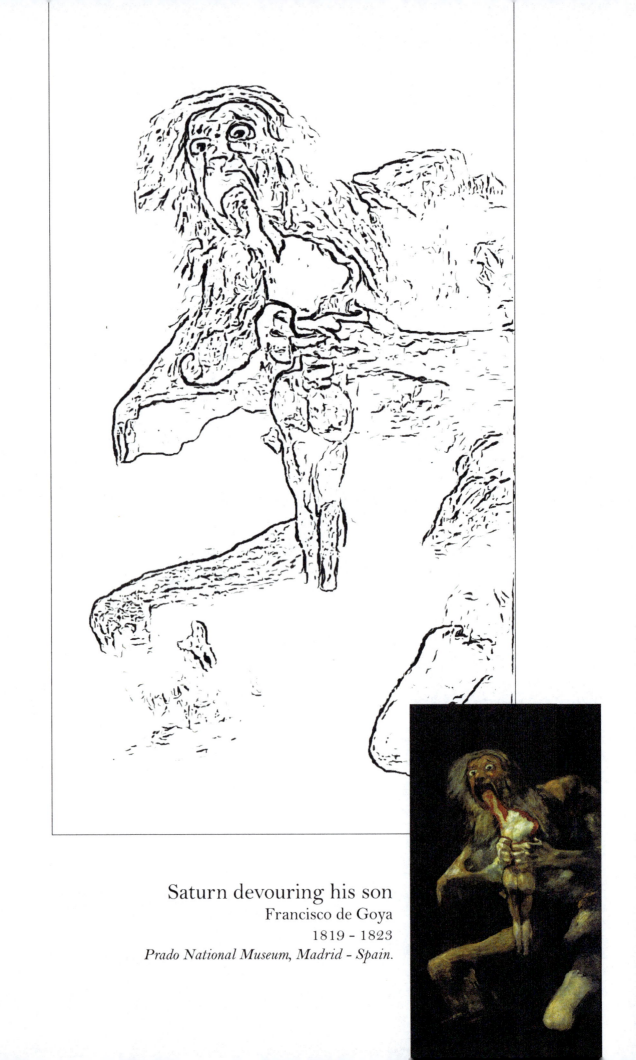

Saturn devouring his son
Francisco de Goya
1819 - 1823
Prado National Museum, Madrid - Spain.

The liberty leading the people
Eugène Delacroix
1830
Louvre Museum, Paris - France.

The great wave off Kanagawa
Katsushika Hokusai
1831
Metropolitan Museum of Art, New York - United States.

The Angelus
Jean-François Millet
1857-1859
Orsay Museum, Paris - France.

The Kiss
Francesco Hayez
1859
Brera Art Gallery, Milan - Italy.

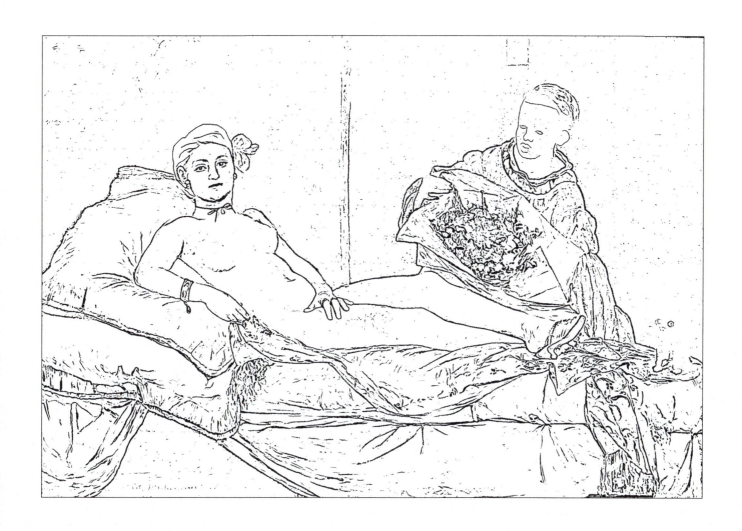

Olympia
Édouard Manet
1863
Orsay Museum, Paris - France.

The birth of Venus
Alexandre Cabanel
1863
Orsay Museum, Paris - France.

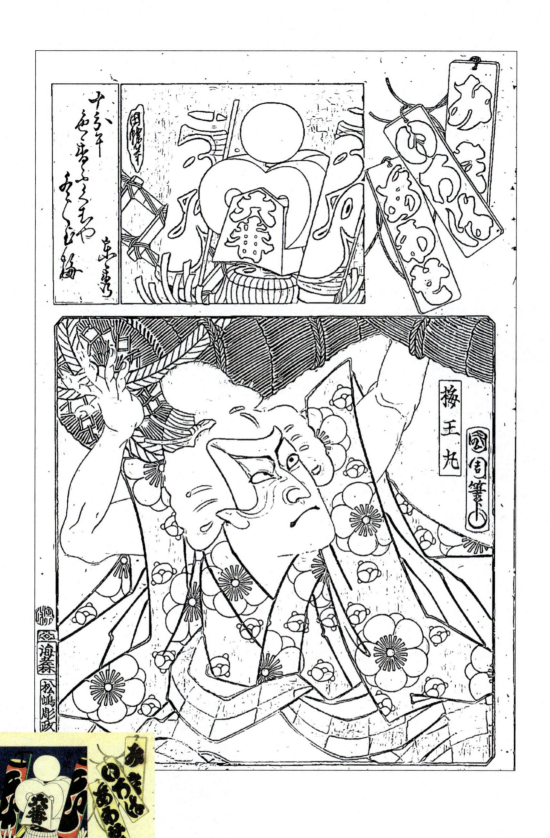

Mu Brigade, 6th Group (Rokubangumi)
Artista desconocido
1866
National Museum of Asian Art, Washington - United States.

Whistler's Mother
James McNeill Whistler
1871
Orsay Museum, Paris - France.

A cotton office in New Orleans
Edgar Degas
1873
Museum of Fine Arts of Pau, France.

45

Paris street in rainy weather
Gustave Caillebotte
1877
Art Institute of Chicago, United States.

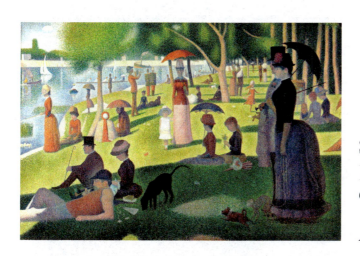

Sunday afternoon on the Island of La Grande Jatte
Georges Pierre Seurat
1884–1886
Art Institute of Chicago, United States.

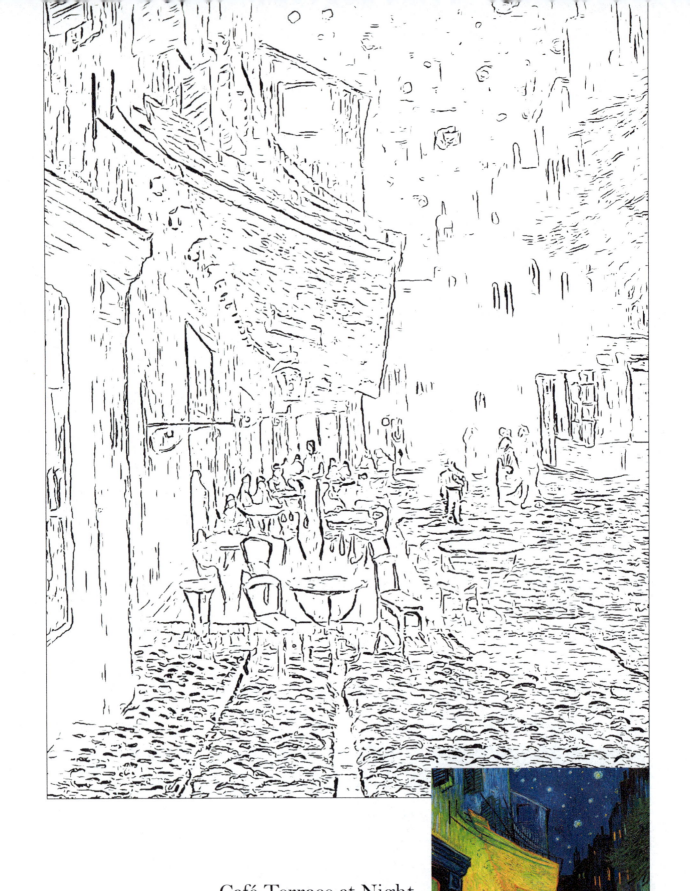

Café Terrace at Night
Vincent van Gogh
1888
Kröller-Müller Museum, The Netherlands.

The starry night
Vincent van Gogh
1889
*Museum of Modern Art (MoMA),
New York - United States.*

49

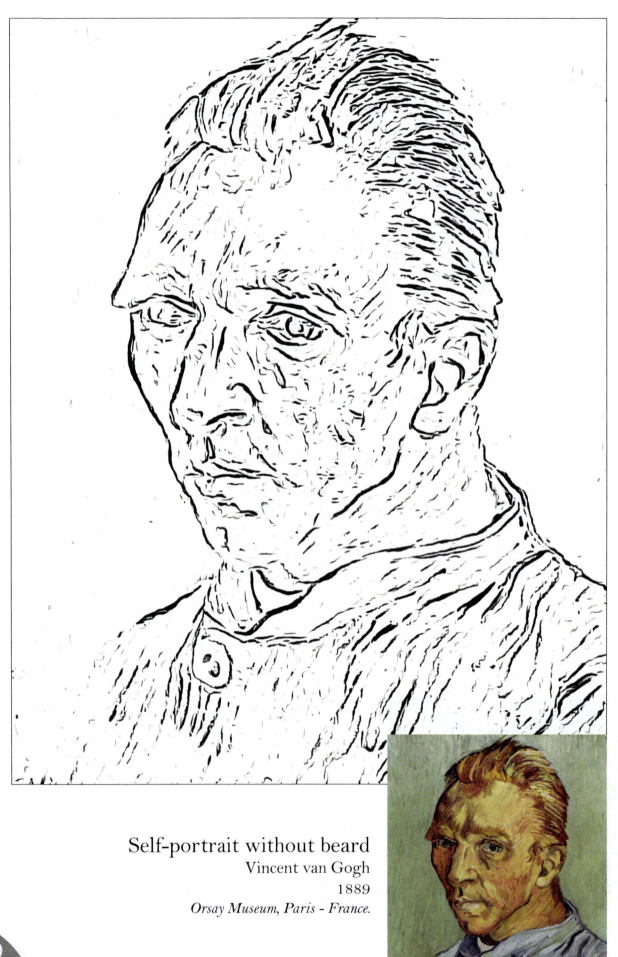

Self-portrait without beard
Vincent van Gogh
1889
Orsay Museum, Paris - France.

50

The scream
Edvard Munch
1893
National Gallery of Norway, Oslo - Norway.

51

Flaming June
Frederic Leighton
1895
Museum of Art of Ponce, Puerto Rico.

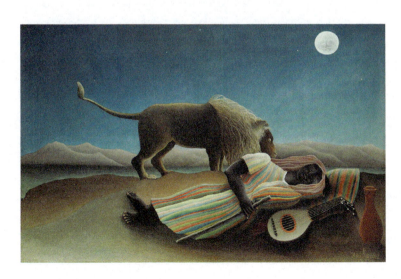

The sleeping gypsy
Henri Rousseau
1897
Museum of Modern Art (MoMA), New York - United States.

Large bathers
Paul Cézanne
1898
Philadelphia Museum of Art, United States.

A friend in need
Cassius Marcellus Coolidge
1903
Chrysler Museum of Art, Norfolk, United States.

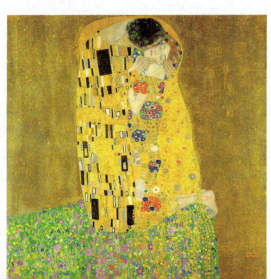

The kiss
Gustav Klimt
1907–1908
Belvedere Gallery, Vienna - Austria.

Les demoiselles d'Avignon
Pablo Picasso
1907
Museum of Modern Art (MoMA), New York - United States.

Foxes
Franz Marc
1913
Private collection.

Three Musicians
Pablo Picasso
1921
Museum of Modern Art (MoMA), New York - United States.

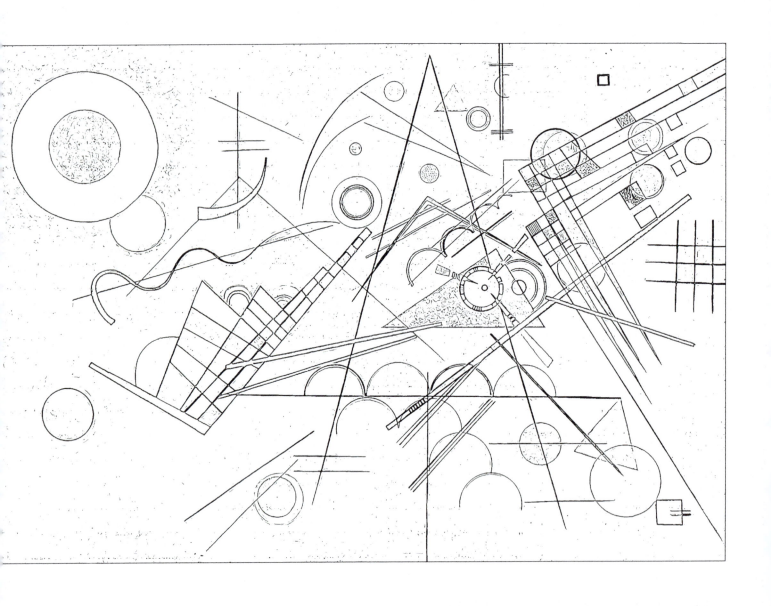

Composition VIII
Vasili Kandinski
1923
Solomon R. Guggenheim Museum, New York - United States.

American gothic
Grant Wood
1930
Art Institute of Chicago, United States.

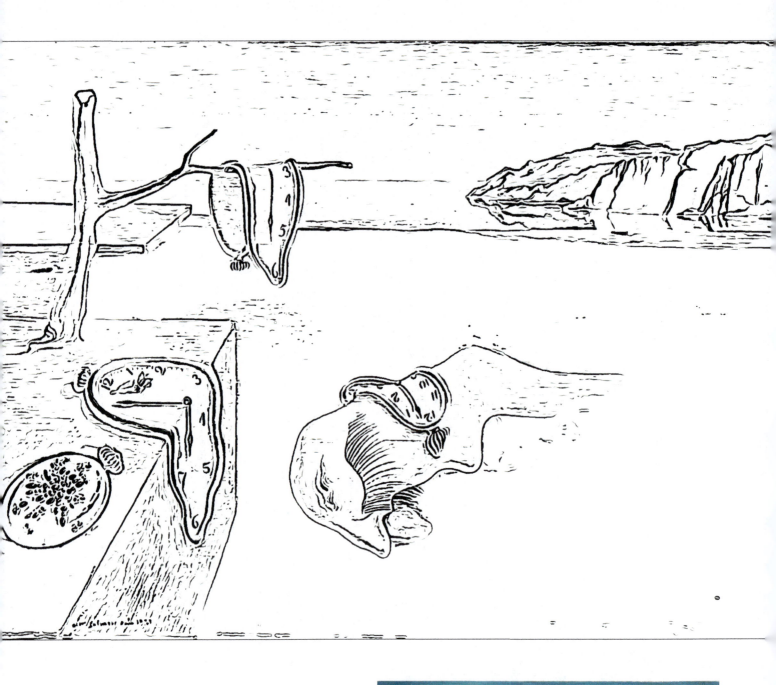

The persistence of memory
Salvador Dalí
1931
Museum of Modern Art (MoMA), New York - United States.

The weeping woman
Pablo Picasso
1937
*British National Museum of Modern Art,
London - United Kingdom.*

The two Fridas
Frida Kahlo
1939
Museum of Modern Art of Mexico City, Mexico.

Nighthawks
Edward Hopper
1942
Art Institute of Chicago, United States.

65

The Temptation of St. Anthony
Salvador Dalí
1946
Royal Museums of Fine Arts of Belgium, Brussels - Belgium.

Shot Marilyns
Andy Warhol
1964
*Metropolitan Museum of Art,
New York - United States.*

The son of man
René Magritte
1964
Private collection.

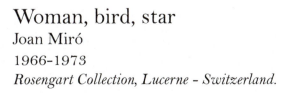

Woman, bird, star
Joan Miró
1966-1973
Rosengart Collection, Lucerne - Switzerland.

Dancers at the Bar
Fernando Botero
2001
Botero Museum, Bogota - Colombia.

Great Works of Art Coloring Book by Arthwr Bass offers more than 60 of the world's most famous paintings to develop creativity and encourage relaxation.

Each page includes the painting in color for reference and relevant information such as the artist, year of creation, and current location.

Some works of art include:
- Maa'at, egyptian goddess of truth.
- Eurynome, pothos , hippodamia, eros, iaso, and asteria.
- Adoration of the magi.
- The Arnolfini portrait.
- St. George and the dragon.
- Annunciation.
- Allegory of spring.
- The birth of venus.
- The last supper.
- The lady with the ermine.
- Mona lisa.
- The creation of adam.
- Triumph of galatea.
- Bacchus and ariadne.
- The (little) tower of Babel.
- The burial of the count of orgaz.
- Musicians.
- Still life with game fowl.
- Susanna and the elders.
- The laughing cavalier.
- Charles i in three positions.
- Las meninas.
- The girl with a pearl earring.
- Mr. And mrs. Andrews.
- The happy accidents of the swing.
- The ladies waldegrave.
- Portrait of a gentleman skating.
- Napoleon crossing the alps.
- Grande odalisque.
- The wanderer above the sea of fog.
- Saturn devouring his son.
- The liberty leading the people.
- The great wave off kanagawa.
- The angelus.
- The kiss.
- Olympia.
- The birth of Venus.
- Mu brigade, 6th group (Rokubangumi).
- Whistler's mother.
- A cotton office in New Orleans.
- Paris street in rainy weather.
- Sunday afternoon on the island of la grande jatte.
- Café terrace at night.
- The starry night.
- Self-portrait without beard.
- The scream.
- Flaming june.
- The sleeping gypsy.
- Large bathers.
- A friend in need.
- The kiss.
- Les demoiselles d'Avignon.
- Foxes.
- Three musicians.
- Composition VIII.
- American gothic.
- The persistence of memory.
- The weeping woman.
- The two Fridas .
- Nighthawks.
- The temptation of st. Anthony.
- Shot marilyns.
- The son of man.
- Woman, bird, star.
- Dancers at the bar.